Anonymus

Acceleration of the Irish Day Mails

Minutes of Evidence

Anonymus

Acceleration of the Irish Day Mails
Minutes of Evidence

ISBN/EAN: 9783741197284

Manufactured in Europe, USA, Canada, Australia, Japa

Cover: Foto ©Thomas Meinert / pixelio.de

Manufactured and distributed by brebook publishing software
(www.brebook.com)

Anonymus

Acceleration of the Irish Day Mails

COMMITTEE ON IRISH DAY MAILS.

MINUTES OF EVIDENCE

TAKEN BEFORE THE

COMMITTEE

APPOINTED BY THE TREASURY TO ENQUIRE INTO THE ACCELERATION

OF THE

IRISH DAY MAILS

WITH

APPENDICES AND INDEX.

Presented to both Houses of Parliament by Command of Her Majesty.

LONDON:
PRINTED FOR HER MAJESTY'S STATIONERY OFFICE,
BY WYMAN AND SONS, LIMITED, FETTER LANE, E.C.

And to be purchased, either directly or through any Bookseller, from
EYRE AND SPOTTISWOODE, East Harding Street, Fleet Street, E.C., and
32, Abingdon Street, Westminster, S.W.; or
JOHN MENZIES & Co., 12, Hanover Street, Edinburgh, and
90, West Nile Street, Glasgow; or
HODGES, FIGGIS & Co., Limited, 104, Grafton Street, Dublin.

LIST OF APPENDICES.

LIST OF WITNESSES.

Tuesday, 14 *December* 1897.

Mr. Edward Watson

Wednesday, 15 *December* 1897.

Mr. Thomas Pye and Mr. John Mooney

Thursday, 16 *December* 1897.

Mr. W. T. Green

Wednesday, 12 *January* 1898.

Mr. W. P. [illegible]
Mr. H. W. [illegible]
Mr. T. F. [illegible]
Mr. G. A. Oakeshott
Mr. Edward Watson
Mr. E. P. [illegible]

Thursday, 13 *January* 1898.

Mr. R. O. [illegible]
Mr. Henry [illegible]
Mr. F. P. E. [illegible]
Mr. [illegible]
The Earl of Kimberley, K.G.
Mr. J. C. [illegible]

Friday, 14 *January* 1898.

Mr. F. P. E. [illegible]
Mr. F. W. [illegible] and Mr. John [illegible]
Mr. W. P. [illegible]
Mr. J. K. [illegible] and Mr. W. H. [illegible]
Mr. [illegible] Vaughan
Mr. H. [illegible] and Mr. David [illegible]
Mr. F. [illegible]
Mr. G. A. Oakeshott
Mr. [illegible]

Wednesday, 23 *March* 1898.

Mr. Frederick Harrison
The Honourable J. C. Burns

Thursday, 24 *March* 1898.

Mr. Frederick Harrison

Friday, 25 *March* 1898.

Mr. G. A. Oakeshott
Mr. Frederick Harrison

Thursday, 31 *March* 1898.

MINUTES OF EVIDENCE

TAKEN BEFORE THE

COMMITTEE ON IRISH DAY MAILS.

PROPOSED ACCELERATION OF DAY MAILS

AND

ALTERATION OF THE TIME OF DEPARTURE.

[illegible] OF IRISH DAY MAILS:

6. ([illegible]) [illegible]

7. [illegible]

8. [illegible]

9. [illegible]

10. [illegible]

11. [illegible]

12. [illegible]

13. [illegible]

14. [illegible]

15. [illegible]

16. [illegible]

17. [illegible]

18. [illegible]

19. [illegible]

20. [illegible]

21. [illegible]

22. [illegible]

23. [illegible]

24. [illegible]

25. [illegible]

26. [illegible]

27. [illegible]

28. [illegible]

29. [illegible]

30. [illegible]

31. [illegible]

32. [illegible]

33. [illegible]

34. [illegible]

35. [illegible]

36. [illegible]

[illegible] London and North-Western Company [illegible]

[illegible]

[illegible] with the English mails [illegible]

[illegible]

[illegible] In the returns of the [illegible]

[illegible]

[illegible]

SECOND DAY.

Wednesday, 15th December, 1897.

[illegible]

[illegible]

[Mr. [illegible]] I can only speak of my own experience [illegible]

[illegible]

[illegible] that is hardly fair after our [illegible]

[illegible]

THIRD DAY.

Thursday, 16th December, 1897

PRESENT:

Mr. Thomas Robertson (*Chairman*).

Mr. Patrick O'Brien, M.P.
Mr. T. E. [illegible].

Mr. T. L. [illegible].

Mr. H. Hamm, *Secretary*.

Mr. [illegible] Chamber of Commerce [illegible]

[illegible]

[illegible] Kingsbridge [illegible]

[illegible]

[illegible]

[illegible]

Mr. Adam S. [illegible]'s pamphlets (see *Appendix A*, p. 43) were then put in evidence.

FOURTH DAY.

Wednesday, 12th January, 1898.

PRESENT:

Mr. Thomas Robertson (Chairman).

Mr. Patrick O'Brien, M.P.
Mr. T. H. Sutton.

Mr. T. L. Heath.

Mr. H. [illegible], Secretary.

Mr. W. W. [illegible], called, and Examined.

[illegible]

[illegible]

[illegible]

[illegible]

[illegible]

[illegible]

[illegible]

[illegible]

Mr. C. A. [illegible] called ; and Examined.

[illegible]

[illegible]

[illegible] **as this is not the** [illegible]

[illegible]

[illegible]

[illegible]

[illegible]

[illegible]

July	[illegible]	[illegible]	[illegible]
August	[illegible]	August [illegible]	[illegible]
September	[illegible]	September [illegible]	[illegible]
October	[illegible]	October [illegible]	[illegible]
November	[illegible]	November [illegible]	[illegible]
December	[illegible]	December [illegible]	[illegible]

[illegible]

[illegible]

FIFTH DAY.

Thursday, 1[illegible]th January, 18[illegible].

PRESENT:

Mr. THOMAS [illegible] (*Chairman*).

Mr. PATRICK O'BRIEN, M.P. | Mr. T. L. HEATH.
Mr. T. E. [illegible]

Mr. [illegible], *Secretary.*

[illegible]

[illegible]

[illegible]

[illegible]

[illegible]

[illegible]

[illegible]

[illegible] a through mileage division [illegible] a pro rata division.

[illegible]

[illegible]
[illegible] Dundalk, [illegible]
[illegible]
[illegible]
[illegible]

[illegible]
[illegible]
[illegible]
[illegible]
[illegible]
[illegible]
[illegible]
[illegible]
[illegible]
[illegible]
[illegible]
[illegible]

[illegible] London, [illegible]
[illegible]
[illegible]
[illegible]

[illegible]

[illegible]

and I see that it is limited down to such an extent that you cannot touch in this inquiry the most vital part affecting the welfare of the country.

[illegible] (*Chairman.*) We'll have to keep within the scope of the reference. [illegible] from this to London, and the day mail from [illegible]—Would you allow me to touch upon the postal question bearing on the fishing industry?

[illegible]

[illegible] I have told you distinctly we cannot touch anything except what affects the two trains?—That is all.

(*Mr. O'Brien.*) We are limited to the two mails.

(*Chairman.*) And the Secretary has told you in his letter what the reference was.

(*Mr. O'Brien.*) I want to ask you something.

(*Chairman.*) You said you would keep within the reference?—I am anxious to do so.

[illegible] (*Mr. O'Brien.*) One of our main purposes was to [illegible] tourist traffic and induce more people to come up by giving them facilities on the mail train. That was the thing that led up to this Committee. The morning mails from Kingstown and from London are the two principal trains we have to consider, and we are finding [illegible] difficulties in the way of even doing that—[illegible] upon the proper question of the postal service to Ireland.

[illegible] We know that; but we hope in time to get all that remedied. You propose that the mail boat should start at [illegible] in the morning?—Yes.

[illegible] In other words, that when the train arrived from Cork it should go on?—Yes.

[illegible] With or without passengers?—We have nothing to do with passengers. We contend that the [illegible] of the mail is not to be governed by one, two, or three passengers on board the boat. We contend that we are entitled to a proper mail service, which will develop the interests of the country.

[illegible] Oh, then, of course it is idle to follow the matter any further, because if you are not willing to run the mail service that is [illegible] to accommodate tourists you will drive them out of the country?—We do; we are anxious to accommodate them.

[illegible] What tourists do you think would go aboard the [illegible] boat or trains in the morning?—I have done so myself. I have more than once knocked about the station from [illegible] to 7, and I have gone so far as to give the porter a tip to let me sit in the carriage for hours to go on by the train.

[illegible] One of the results of our inquiry would be to give you better facilities; are the mail services of which you complain worse now than before May last, when the new service was established?—They are delayed now.

[illegible] You say that the limited mail leaves [illegible] now as it did before May last, and you complain that the train goes away before the English letters come in?—Exactly, the mail train leaving London in the evening being put back, has injured the delivery of the service all over Ireland.

(*Chairman.*) I suggest after that.

[illegible] (*Mr. O'Brien.*) Were you before May last able to catch that limited mail train from [illegible] with answers to letters from England in reply to those which came in by the mid-day train?—[illegible] I allude to the [illegible] districts of [illegible]. It does not affect [illegible]; but a large district of the country. Between [illegible] and [illegible] there are about 1,000 vessels during the season, and I have known £[illegible] paid in one day in [illegible], and these are industries that we want to affect.

(*Chairman.*) I think it would be best for you to put your views in writing and submit them to us, and we can then include all that is legitimate.

The witness then withdrew, upon the understanding that he should attend next morning and submit his views in writing.

[illegible]

[illegible]

[illegible]

[illegible]

[illegible]

SIXTH DAY.

Friday, 14th January, 1898.

PRESENT:

Mr. Thomas [illegible] (Chairman).

Mr. Patrick O'Brien, M.P.
Mr. T. [illegible]

Mr. T. L. [illegible]

Mr. R. [illegible], Secretary.

Mr. P. P. H. [illegible], recalled; and further Examined.

[illegible]

[illegible]

Mr. [illegible], Chairman, and Mr. [illegible] of the Dublin, **Wicklow and Wexford Railway** Company, called; and Examined.

[illegible]

[illegible]

[illegible]

[illegible]

[illegible]

[illegible]

[illegible]

[illegible]

[illegible]

[illegible]

[illegible]

[illegible]

[illegible]

[illegible]

[illegible]

[illegible]

[illegible]

[illegible]

[illegible]

[illegible]

[illegible]

1424. Do you have a good business day of some eight hours. Is not that correspondence delivered in London early each morning?—It is; yes.

1425. Is that a service that ought to be supplemented, at no enormous expenditure, by the turning of the whole of the Irish night mail service?—But even if only, during without the continuation from London, we could go right through Dublin, it would be a great advantage. When a business man comes home, if this change is made, he could reply to a letter, and the people in England can reply to him. He cannot reply now if he does not come home in the middle of the day.—(Mr. Martin.) I frequently get telegrams at five o'clock at night, and I have to wait until five next day, whereas, with a quick night mail, I could post up to ten o'clock.

1426. (Mr. Sexton.) Don't you think when the officers of the Post Office have given you eight hours for replying to English Night Mail letters, you have not much to complain of?—(Mr. Barrett.) I only say if a change is to be made that is one that would help the business.

1427. It would give some additional facilities?—It would in every way. Now a young man in our employment is going to [?], and by carrying out the arrangement I suggest he could be six hours nearer to [?].

1428. (Mr. O'Brien.) Hasn't he a route from Belfast?—Not so good as this. This is a day service.

1429. Isn't there a day service by Greenore?—No.

Mr. T. [illegible], Postmaster and Surveyor, Liverpool, called; and Examined.

[illegible]

[illegible]. Well, [illegible] the [illegible] part [illegible] to Ireland [illegible] to Liverpool [illegible].

[illegible]. Having in view [illegible] you have a night mail [illegible] [illegible] letters in Liverpool [illegible].

[illegible]. The [illegible] of [illegible] [illegible] given by the [illegible] evening [illegible], that is [illegible] the [illegible] [illegible] [illegible] [illegible] [illegible] the [illegible] [illegible] of [illegible] in the [illegible] [illegible] the [illegible] evening.

[illegible]. That is quite a fair [illegible] [illegible] [illegible] [illegible] [illegible] it. Take Dublin, for instance, the [illegible] of the correspondence [illegible] [illegible] [illegible] [illegible] [illegible].

[illegible]. So we should [illegible] it by having a later [illegible]?—Yes.

[illegible]. And what you speak of might be [illegible] by the [illegible] [illegible]?—Yes.

[illegible]. (Mr. O'Brien.) You said, Mr. Shilliday, that the [illegible] [illegible] of Liverpool [illegible] with Ireland? —[illegible] I have no personal knowledge of. But I have [illegible] [illegible] [illegible] [illegible] the information [illegible] [illegible] [illegible] [illegible]; and one of these [illegible] me a few days ago [illegible] [illegible] [illegible] [illegible] [illegible] by [illegible] [illegible] [illegible] [illegible] [illegible] [illegible] Irish [illegible] [illegible]. There was [illegible] [illegible] [illegible] [illegible] Dublin or Belfast.

[illegible]. If you had more knowledge you would not think [illegible]?—I have no personal knowledge.

[illegible]. [illegible] [illegible], [illegible] you are considering a [illegible] [illegible] [illegible] Liverpool [illegible].

[illegible]. [illegible] [illegible] to [illegible] in operation this year?—Not this year.

[illegible]. [illegible] [illegible] [illegible] [illegible] operation it [illegible] [illegible] into the [illegible] of the [illegible].

[illegible]. And [illegible] the [illegible] of [illegible] [illegible] [illegible] [illegible] in trading with Ireland?—That is so.

[illegible]. Therefore, the people there would [illegible] up the Irish letters if [illegible] [illegible] them [illegible] [illegible] [illegible] [illegible] [illegible] [illegible].

[illegible]. Well, [illegible] [illegible] if they [illegible] [illegible]?—Yes.

[illegible]. They [illegible] [illegible] [illegible] by this [illegible] [illegible] the [illegible] of the [illegible], and he said [illegible] [illegible], and [illegible] [illegible] a [illegible] of [illegible] [illegible] [illegible] in the [illegible] in Liverpool.

[illegible]. [illegible] [illegible] [illegible] [illegible] [illegible] [illegible] [illegible] That is the [illegible] of the [illegible]. [illegible] of [illegible] [illegible] [illegible] [illegible] the Exchange.

[illegible]. [illegible] [illegible] [illegible] of [illegible] in [illegible] [illegible]—[illegible] [illegible] [illegible] in the [illegible] [illegible] (and [illegible]), of which I [illegible] the name.

[illegible]. And [illegible] [illegible] [illegible]?—Yes.

[illegible]. [illegible] [illegible] that [illegible] will not get a considerable [illegible] of people [illegible] [illegible] [illegible] the [illegible] [illegible] in Ireland?—[illegible] [illegible] [illegible] of [illegible] [illegible] half the [illegible] [illegible] [illegible] [illegible] [illegible] [illegible] [illegible] [illegible] for delivery [illegible] [illegible] [illegible] and the [illegible] in the [illegible].

[illegible]. [illegible] [illegible] [illegible] [illegible] [illegible] [illegible], the Post Office [illegible] at night, [illegible] [illegible] [illegible] [illegible] [illegible] [illegible].

[illegible]. [illegible] [illegible] [illegible] [illegible] [illegible] the letters [illegible] [illegible] [illegible] [illegible] [illegible].

[illegible]. [illegible] [illegible] [illegible] [illegible] [illegible] your [illegible] [illegible] [illegible] [illegible]?—They [illegible] [illegible] in the bags at [illegible], and [illegible] [illegible] [illegible] [illegible] [illegible] at [illegible]. We [illegible] [illegible] [illegible] of [illegible] [illegible].

[illegible]. Now, if [illegible] [illegible] [illegible] [illegible] [illegible] the line between Holyhead and Liverpool, would [illegible] [illegible] [illegible] [illegible] [illegible] [illegible] [illegible]—[illegible] [illegible] [illegible]: but there would be [illegible] [illegible].

[illegible]. Very well, your [illegible] [illegible] [illegible] [illegible] [illegible] [illegible] [illegible] [illegible] [illegible] [illegible] the [illegible]?—[illegible] [illegible] [illegible] [illegible] [illegible] [illegible] [illegible] [illegible] [illegible] [illegible] [illegible] [illegible] [illegible] [illegible] [illegible] the [illegible]. The [illegible] [illegible] [illegible] [illegible] [illegible] the delivery [illegible] [illegible]; [illegible] a number of [illegible] [illegible] [illegible] [illegible] [illegible] [illegible] [illegible] [illegible] [illegible] [illegible] [illegible] [illegible] [illegible] [illegible] [illegible] [illegible] [illegible].

[illegible]. [illegible] [illegible] [illegible] [illegible] [illegible], [illegible] they?—Yes.

[illegible]. What time is [illegible] [illegible] [illegible]?

[illegible]. Well, [illegible] [illegible] [illegible] [illegible] [illegible] [illegible] [illegible] [illegible] [illegible] [illegible] [illegible] [illegible] [illegible] [illegible] [illegible] letters [illegible] of letters to the [illegible] [illegible] [illegible] [illegible] [illegible] [illegible] [illegible] [illegible].

[illegible]. Yes, [illegible] [illegible] [illegible] the people [illegible] [illegible] [illegible] [illegible] [illegible] [illegible] [illegible] [illegible] [illegible] [illegible]. They [illegible] [illegible] [illegible] [illegible]. Mr. [illegible] Shilliday. [illegible] [illegible]

[illegible]. [illegible] [illegible] [illegible] any difficulty in [illegible] delivery and the [illegible] [illegible] [illegible].

[illegible]. [illegible] [illegible] [illegible] [illegible] [illegible]?—No.

[illegible]. You [illegible] [illegible] [illegible] the bags to your office?—Yes.

[illegible]. And [illegible] [illegible] [illegible] [illegible] [illegible] by the [illegible].

[illegible]. And [illegible] [illegible] [illegible] [illegible] [illegible] [illegible] [illegible] [illegible] [illegible] [illegible] [illegible]?—[illegible] [illegible] [illegible] [illegible] [illegible] [illegible] [illegible] [illegible] [illegible] [illegible] [illegible] [illegible] [illegible] [illegible] [illegible].

[illegible]. And that [illegible] [illegible] [illegible] [illegible] [illegible] [illegible] [illegible] [illegible] [illegible] [illegible] [illegible]?—Not [illegible] [illegible] [illegible] [illegible] [illegible] [illegible] [illegible] [illegible] [illegible].

[illegible]. [illegible] [illegible] [illegible] [illegible] [illegible] [illegible] Liverpool [illegible] [illegible] [illegible] [illegible] [illegible] [illegible] [illegible] [illegible] [illegible] [illegible] [illegible].

[illegible]. [illegible] [illegible] [illegible] [illegible] [illegible] [illegible] [illegible] [illegible] [illegible] [illegible] [illegible] [illegible] [illegible] [illegible] [illegible] [illegible] [illegible].

[illegible]. [illegible] I [illegible] [illegible] [illegible] [illegible] [illegible] [illegible] [illegible] [illegible] [illegible] [illegible] [illegible] [illegible] [illegible] [illegible] [illegible] [illegible] Liverpool, [illegible] [illegible].

[illegible]. [illegible]—The [illegible] [illegible] [illegible] Liverpool [illegible].

[illegible]. [illegible], [illegible] [illegible] [illegible] of English [illegible] [illegible] [illegible] [illegible] [illegible] [illegible] [illegible] [illegible] service?—[illegible] [illegible] [illegible] [illegible].

[illegible]. [illegible] English [illegible] [illegible] [illegible] [illegible] [illegible] [illegible] [illegible] [illegible] [illegible] [illegible] [illegible] [illegible] England [illegible] [illegible] [illegible] [illegible] [illegible] [illegible] Ireland [illegible] [illegible].

[illegible]. (Mr. [illegible].) [illegible] [illegible] of this question as to [illegible] [illegible] Liverpool, [illegible] [illegible] [illegible] [illegible] [illegible] Liverpool [illegible] [illegible] [illegible] delivery [illegible] Liverpool Post Office [illegible] [illegible] [illegible] [illegible] [illegible] [illegible] [illegible].

[illegible]. It could be done if Liverpool [illegible] [illegible] [illegible] [illegible]?—Yes.

[illegible]. [illegible] [illegible] [illegible] [illegible] [illegible] [illegible] [illegible] should make [illegible] [illegible] [illegible] for [illegible]?—[illegible] [illegible] [illegible] Liverpool [illegible] [illegible] [illegible] [illegible] [illegible] [illegible] [illegible] [illegible] [illegible] [illegible] [illegible] [illegible] Manchester and Birmingham [illegible] [illegible] [illegible] [illegible].

[illegible]. [illegible] [illegible] [illegible] [illegible] [illegible] it would be possible [illegible] [illegible] [illegible] [illegible] [illegible] [illegible] [illegible] [illegible] [illegible] [illegible] [illegible] [illegible] Post Office; [illegible] [illegible] [illegible] [illegible] [illegible] [illegible] [illegible], it would [illegible] [illegible].

[illegible]. It is [illegible] [illegible] [illegible] [illegible] [illegible] [illegible] [illegible] [illegible] [illegible] [illegible] [illegible] [illegible] [illegible] [illegible] [illegible] [illegible].

[illegible]. (Mr. O'Brien.) You are a [illegible] [illegible] in the [illegible]?—Over thirty years.

[illegible]. You [illegible].

[illegible]. [illegible], [illegible] the public are getting [illegible] [illegible] [illegible]?—Yes.

[illegible]. [illegible].

[illegible]. [illegible] [illegible] [illegible] [illegible] [illegible] [illegible] [illegible] [illegible] [illegible] [illegible] [illegible] [illegible] [illegible] [illegible] [illegible] [illegible] [illegible] [illegible] Liverpool [illegible] [illegible] [illegible] [illegible] [illegible] [illegible] [illegible] [illegible] [illegible] [illegible] [illegible] [illegible] [illegible] [illegible] letters [illegible] [illegible].

[illegible]

Mr. G. A. [illegible], recalled; and further Examined.

[illegible]

[illegible]

Examination of Mr. D. Gore, C.E., Engineer to the Board of Public Works.

[illegible]

SEVENTH DAY.

Wednesday, 23rd March, 1886.

PRESENT:

Mr. [illegible] (*Chairman*).

Mr. Patrick O'Brien, M.P.
Mr. T. E. [illegible]

Mr. T. L. Heath.

Mr. H. [illegible], *Secretary.*

Mr. Frederick Harrison, General Manager of the London and North-Western **Railway Company,** called and Examined.

[illegible]

[illegible]

[illegible]

[illegible]

[illegible]

[illegible]

[illegible] The North-Western Company may probably be charged for a [illegible]

[illegible]

[illegible]

[illegible]

[illegible]

[illegible]

[illegible]

EIGHTH DAY

Thursday, 24th March, 1898.

PRESENT:

[illegible]

[illegible]

[illegible]

[illegible]

[illegible]

[illegible]

NINTH DAY.

Friday, 25th March, 1898.

PRESENT:

Mr. THOMAS [illegible] (*Chairman*).

Mr. PATRICK O'BRIEN, M.P. | Mr. T. L. HEATH.
Mr. T. E. [illegible].

Mr. H. [illegible], *Secretary*.

[illegible]

[illegible]

[illegible]

TENTH DAY.

Thursday, 31st March, 18[illegible].

PRESENT:

Mr. THOMAS ROBERTSON (*Chairman*).

[illegible]

[illegible]

[illegible]
bags.
arrives at the Post Office
Compton Street, do you
of the mail?—Practically
to be sorted, because they
send them on by the [illegible]

have you any margin to
in the Office, certainly

the interval by fifteen

[illegible]

[illegible]

[illegible]

APPENDIX.

Appendix A.

APPENDIX A.

[illegible]

[illegible]

"Yours, &c.,
"A. [illegible]."

Copy of Letter [illegible] by Mr. [illegible] to each of the Irish Members of Parliament.

[illegible]

"THE ACCELERATION OF THE IRISH MAILS.

"Dear Sir,

[illegible]

Copy of a Letter which appeared in the Irish Times, [illegible] September, 189[illegible].

[illegible]

"THE MAILS ACCELERATION.

"Sir,

[illegible]

Appendix A.

June 3rd, 1897."

APPENDIX B.

[illegible]

"Henry Higgs, Esq.,
"Secretary, Day Mail Committee."

APPENDIX C.

[illegible]

"London and North Western Railway, [illegible]

[illegible]

(Signed) [illegible]

"Thomas Robertson, Esq., [illegible]

APPENDIX D.

[illegible]

(Signed) [illegible]
Secretary."

"Thomas Robertson, Esq.,
"Chairman, Board of Public Works."

ANALYSIS OF EVIDENCE.

AUSTIN, Mr. H. W., Stenographic Clerk, [illegible], Dublin:
[illegible]

BADCOCK, Mr. J. C., Controller, London Postal Service:
[illegible]

[illegible], Mr. T., and [illegible], Mr. T., [illegible] Chamber of Commerce:
[illegible]

[illegible], Mr. T. [illegible], Surveyor, Northern District, Ireland:
[illegible]

[illegible], Mr. J. [illegible], and [illegible], Mr. W. H., Londonderry Chamber of Commerce:
[illegible]

[illegible]:
[illegible]

COGHLAN, Mr. J. (See PIM, Mr. F. W.)

[illegible], Mr. R. C., Manager Great Southern and Western Railway:
[illegible]

[illegible], Mr. [illegible], Surveyor, North Wales District:
[illegible]

[illegible], Mr. W. P.:
[illegible]

[illegible], Mr. W. T., ex-President Chamber of Commerce, Cork:
[illegible]

[illegible], Mr. W. T.—continued:
[illegible]

[illegible], Mr. B. C. K., Engineer Board of Public Works:
[illegible]

HARRISON, Mr. Frederick, General Manager London and North Western Railway:
[illegible]

KILMOREY, Earl of, K.P.:
[illegible]

[illegible], Mr. D. (See BADCOCK, Mr. J. C.)

[illegible], Mr. W. H. (See [illegible], Mr. J. E.)

[illegible], Mr. J., Dublin Chamber of Commerce:
[illegible]

[illegible], Mr. G. A., Secretary's Office, General Post Office, London:
[illegible]

PIM, Mr. F. W., Dublin, Wicklow and Wexford Railway:
[illegible]

[illegible], Mr. [illegible], [illegible]:
[illegible]

[illegible], Mr. [illegible], Manager, Great Northern Railway of Ireland:
[illegible]

[illegible], Mr. [illegible]:
[illegible]

[illegible], Mr. W. P., Controller of [illegible] Office, Dublin:
[illegible]

[illegible], Mr. F., [illegible]:
[illegible]

[illegible], Mr. [illegible]—continued:
[illegible]

[illegible], Mr. E. F., [illegible] Company:
[illegible]

[illegible], Mr. J., Manager, [illegible] Railway of Ireland:
[illegible]

[illegible], Mr. F., Manager, [illegible] Railway:
[illegible]

[illegible], Mr [illegible], City of Dublin [illegible] Company:
[illegible]

[illegible]

www.ingramcontent.com/pod-product-compliance
Lightning Source LLC
Chambersburg PA
CBHW020252290326
41930CB00039B/836
* 9 7 8 3 7 4 1 1 9 7 2 8 4 *